THIS BOOK
BELONGS TO

_____

HOW TO USE

THIS BOOK...

The season of Lent gives us an opportunity to really reflect on our relationship with both Christ and each other. Sometimes we think that we have to make HUGE sacrifices to do this. However, even in the small reflections, we still can learn to love Jesus more fully and joyfully.

This book asks only one question a day.

One question a day to help you reflect on who you are, who your friends are, and who God is.
One question a day to help you really look at your life to reflect on if it is the life God wants you to lead.
One question a day to help you reflect on how, during this season of Lent, you can better your relationship with yourself, your friends and family, and God.

Once you're finished reflecting on each day's question, take an opportunity to offer a prayer for people in our world who really need it. It doesn't have to be anything fancy, just a request to God to give them some grace and to continue loving them.

During this season of Lent, remember that saints did not get to heaven by doing extraordinary things. They simply did all things, big and little, with love.

Consider these next 40 days ones to make you stronger, wiser, and more faithful! Also, remember that Sundays are not included on your question a day list, so use them as a day to rest or get caught up if you miss a day!

May our God continue to do wonderful things through you!

W	T	F	S	M
T	W	T	F	S
M	T	W	T	F
S	M	T	W	T
F	S	M	T	W
T	F	S	M	T
W	T	F	S	M
T	W	T	F	S

ALL GO TO ONE PLACE; ALL ARE FROM THE DUST, AND ALL TURN TO DUST AGAIN.

Ecclesiastes 3:20

Today's Question

Are you embarrassed to wear your ashes today? Why or why not?

_____

_____

_____

_____

_____

_____

_____

_____

Today's Prayer Request

Your parish priest.

"GOD NEVER TIRES OF FORGIVING US; WE ARE THE ONES WHO TIRE OF SEEKING HIS MERCY."

Pope Francis

Today's Question

Where do you stand in your relationship
with God right now?

_____

_____

_____

_____

_____

_____

_____

_____

_____

Today's Prayer Request

Your teacher.

"APART FROM THE CROSS, THERE IS NO OTHER LADDER BY WHICH WE MAY GO TO HEAVEN."

St. Rose of Lima

Today's Question

Do you ever doubt there is a heaven?
Why or why not?

_____

_____

_____

_____

_____

_____

_____

_____

Today's Prayer Request

Someone who is sick.

"MANY ARE THE PLANS IN A PERSON'S HEART, BUT IT IS THE LORD'S PURPOSE THAT PREVAILS."

Proverbs 19:21

Today's Question

What do you think God's plan for you is?

_____

_____

_____

_____

_____

_____

_____

_____

Today's Prayer Request

Your best friend.

"LENTEN FASTS MAKE M
FEEL BETTER, STRONGER
AND MORE ACTIVE THAN
EVER."

St. Catherine of Genoa

Today's Question

What is your lenten promise this year?
How is it going?

_____

_____

_____

_____

_____

_____

_____

_____

Today's Prayer Request

Your neighbor.

"THEN THE LORD GOD FORMED A MAN FROM THE DUST OF THE GROUND AND BREATHED INTO HIS NOSTRILS THE BREATH OF LIFE, AND THE MAN BECAME A LIVING BEING."

Genesis 2:7

Today's Question

What makes you feel truly alive? Explain the feeling.

_____

_____

_____

_____

_____

_____

_____

_____

Today's Prayer Request

Your mom and dad.

"YET EVEN NOW, SAYS THE LORD, RETURN TO ME WITH ALL YOUR HEART, WITH FASTING, WITH WEEPING, AND WITH MOURNING"

Joel 2:12

Today's Question

If Jesus was standing in front of you, how would you respond?

_____

_____

_____

_____

_____

_____

_____

_____

Today's Prayer Request

Someone who is lonely.

"WE MUST TRUST IN THE MIGHTY POWER OF GOD'S MERCY. WE ARE ALL SINNERS, BUT HIS GRACE TRANSFORMS US AND MAKES US NEW."

Pope Benedict XVI

Today's Question

When was the last time you went to reconciliation? Describe the experience.

_____

_____

_____

_____

_____

_____

_____

_____

_____

Today's Prayer Request

Our world leaders.

"ARE YOU CAPABLE OF RISKING YOUR LIFE FOR SOMEONE? DO IT FOR CHRIST."

St. John Paul II

Today's Question

Have you ever been embarrassed to talk about your faith to someone? Describe the experience.

_____

_____

_____

_____

_____

_____

_____

Today's Prayer Request

A new kid at school.

"WHILE THE WORLD CHANGES, THE CROSS STANDS FIRM."

St. Bruno

Today's Question

What does the cross represent to you?

_____

_____

_____

_____

_____

_____

_____

Today's Prayer Request

Your Grandparents

"JESUS TELLS ME THAT I LOVE IT IS HE WHO DELIGHTS ME; IN SUFFERING, ON THE OTHER HAND, IT IS I WHO DELIGHT HIM."

St.Padre Pio

Today's Question

What has been really hard lately? Explain why you are struggling with it.

_____

_____

_____

_____

_____

_____

_____

_____

Today's Prayer Request

Your Classmates.

"DO NOT BE ANXIOUS ABOUT ANYTHING, BUT IN EVERYTHING, BY PRAYER AND PETITION, WITH THANKSGIVING, PRESENT YOUR REQUESTS TO GOD.

Philippians 4:6

Today's Question

What is your biggest fear?

_____

_____

_____

_____

_____

_____

_____

Today's Prayer Request

Someone who is suffering.

"START BY DOING WHAT IS NECESSARY THEN DO WHAT IS POSSIBLE AND SUDDENLY YOU ARE DOING THE IMPOSSIBLE."

St. Francis of Assisi

Today's Question

What did you procrastinate today?

_____

_____

_____

_____

_____

_____

_____

Today's Prayer Request

Your own personal intention.

"DON'T WASTE YOUR SUFFERING."

St. John Paul II

Today's Question

Who is someone who could really use your prayers?

_____

_____

_____

_____

_____

_____

_____

_____

Today's Prayer Request

Someone who had a hard day.

"WHOEVER DOES NOT LOVE DOES NOT KNOW GOD, FOR GOD IS LOVE."

1 John 4:8

Today's Question

Who showed you love unexpectedly today?

_____

_____

_____

_____

_____

_____

_____

_____

Today's Prayer Request

Your school principal.

"ASK, AND IT WILL BE GIVEN YOU; SEARCH, AND YOU WILL FIND; KNOCK, AND THE DOOR WILL BE OPENED FOR YOU."

Matthew 7:7

Today's Question

What is one question you really wish God would answer for you right now?

_____

_____

_____

_____

_____

_____

_____

_____

Today's Prayer Request

All doctors and nurses.

"LENT IS A GOOD TIME FOR SACRIFICING. LET US DENY OURSELVES SOMETHING EVERY DAY TO HELP OTHERS."

Pope Francis

Today's Question

What is the last thing you've sacrificed to better someone else?

_____

_____

_____

_____

_____

_____

_____

_____

Today's Prayer Request

Someone who has passed away.

"GIVE SOMETHING HOWEVER SMALL, TO THE ONE IN NEED. FOR IT IS NOT SMALL TO ONE WHO HAS NOTHING. NEITHER IS IT SMALL TO GOD, IF WE HAVE GIVEN WHAT WE COULD."

St. Gregory Nazianzen

Today's Question

What is your most cherished possession that has been given to you?

_____

_____

_____

_____

_____

_____

_____

_____

Today's Prayer Request

The Pope

"THE WORLD'S THY SHIP AND NOT THY HOME."

St. Therese of Lisieux

Today's Question

Where have you been focusing most of your attention lately? Why has this been important to you?

_____

_____

_____

_____

_____

_____

_____

Today's Prayer Request

Someone who is homeless.

"CREATE IN ME A CLEAN HEART, O GOD, AND PUT A NEW AND RIGHT SPIRI WITHIN ME."

Psalm 51:10

Today's Question

Who has made you mad lately? Explain
the situation.

_____

_____

_____

_____

_____

_____

_____

Today's Prayer Request

Someone who has hurt your feelings

"JESUS LOOKED AT THEM AND SAID, "FOR MORTALS IT IS IMPOSSIBLE, BUT NOT FOR GOD; FOR GOD ALL THINGS ARE POSSIBLE."

Mark 10:27

Today's Question

If you could ask God to do anything for you, what would you ask Him to do?

_____

_____

_____

_____

_____

_____

_____

_____

Today's Prayer Request

All police

"REAL FASTING IS NOT MERELY AN ABSTINENCE FROM MEATS, BUT FROM SINS TOO."

St. John Chrysostom

Today's Question

What is a sin that you really struggle with?

_____

_____

_____

_____

_____

_____

_____

Today's Prayer Request

Everyone in the military.

"JESUS SAID TO HIM, "I AM THE WAY, AND THE TRUTH, AND THE LIFE. NO ONE COMES TO THE FATHER EXCEPT THROUGH ME."

John 14:6

Today's Question

How is your prayer routine? What needs changing?

_____

_____

_____

_____

_____

_____

_____

_____

Today's Prayer Request

Someone who feels left out.

"DO NOT FEAR, FOR I AM WITH YOU, DO NOT BE AFRAID, FOR I AM YOUR GOD; I WILL STRENGTHEN YOU, I WILL HELP YOU, I WILL UPHOLD YOU WITH MY VICTORIOUS RIGHT HAND."

Isaiah 41:10

Today's Question

What scares you from trusting God fully?

_____

_____

_____

_____

_____

_____

_____

_____

Today's Prayer Request

A new friend.

"LENT COMES PROVIDENTIALLY TO REAWAKEN US, TO SHAKE US FROM OUR LETHARGY."

Pope Francis

Today's Question

Where does your daily routine need changing? How can you change it to be the best you can be?

_____

_____

_____

_____

_____

_____

_____

Today's Prayer Request

Someone living in a dangerous place.

"PRAYER IS IN FACT THE RECOGNITION OF OUR LIMITS AND OUR DEPENDENCE: WE COME FROM GOD, WE ARE OF GOD, AND TO GOD WE RETURN."

St. John Paul II

Today's Question

What is a prayer you were shocked to find out was answered?

_____

_____

_____

_____

_____

_____

_____

_____

Today's Prayer Request

Senior citizens who feel lonely.

"PRAYER IS BEING ON TERMS OF FRIENDSHIP WITH GOD, FREQUENTLY CONVERSING IN SECRET WITH HIM WHO, WE KNOW, LOVES US."

St. Theresa of Avila

Today's Question

How often do you pray? What does this
prayer consist of?

_____

_____

_____

_____

_____

_____

_____

_____

Today's Prayer Request

Your Godparents.

"THE SAINTS DID NOT ALL BEGIN WELL, BUT THEY ALL ENDED WELL."

St. John Vianney

Today's Question

Who is a saint you really admire? Explain
why you've chosen them.

_____

_____

_____

_____

_____

_____

_____

_____

Today's Prayer Request

Someone suffering with mental illness.

"HE CAME TO LEAD OUR LIVES AWAY FROM CORRUPTION TO HIMSEL AND GAVE US FREEDOM IN PLACE OF SLAVERY."

St. Anastasius II of Antioch

Today's Question

What do you feel enslaved by? Give an
example of how you feel.

_____

_____

_____

_____

_____

_____

_____

_____

Today's Prayer Request

A volunteer at your church.

"HOLINESS DOES NOT CONSIST IN DOING EXTRAORDINARY THINGS. IT CONSISTS IN ACCEPTING, WITH A SMILE, WHAT JESUS SENDS US. IT CONSISTS IN ACCEPTING AND FOLLOWING THE WILL OF GOD."

St. Theresa of Calcutta

Today's Question

When was the last time you took your anger out on someone who didn't deserve it? Explain the situation.

_____

_____

_____

_____

_____

_____

_____

Today's Prayer Request

A classmate you don't really speak to.

"WORK AS IF EVERYTHING DEPENDED ON YOU, PRAY AS IF EVERYTHING DEPENDED ON GOD."

St. Ignatius of Loyola

Today's Question

Who do you feel you rely on more;
yourself or God? Explain why you feel this
way.

_____

_____

_____

_____

_____

_____

_____

Today's Prayer Request

All firefighters.

"JESUS IS WITH YOU EVEN WHEN YOU DON'T FEEL HIS PRESENCE. HE IS NEVER SO CLOSE TO YOU AS HE IS DURING YOUR SPIRITUAL BATTLES."

St. Padre Pio

Today's Question

Where do you feel Jesus' presence in your day?

_____

_____

_____

_____

_____

_____

_____

_____

Today's Prayer Request

Someone you miss.

"I HAVE SAID THIS TO YOU, SO THAT IN ME YOU MAY HAVE PEACE. IN THE WORLD YOU FACE PERSECUTION. BUT TAKE COURAGE; I HAVE CONQUERED THE WORLD!"

John 16:33

Today's Question

Where do you go to find peace? Describe
why this place is peaceful to you.

_____

_____

_____

_____

_____

_____

_____

_____

Today's Prayer Request

Someone who is trying to get a better job

"DARKNESS CAN ONLY BE SCATTERED BY LIGHT, HATRED CAN ONLY BE CONQUERED BY LOVE."

St. John Paul II

Today's Question

Are you or have you ever been scared of the dark? If yes, how do you conquer the fear?

_____

_____

_____

_____

_____

_____

_____

Today's Prayer Request

All paramedics.

"WE BECOME WHAT WE LOVE AND WHO WE LOVE SHAPES WHAT WE BECOME."

St.Claire of Assisi

Today's Question

Who is a person in your life that people compare you to? Do you like to be compared to this person? Why or why not?

_____

_____

_____

_____

_____

_____

_____

Today's Prayer Request

Someone who needs a break.

"WHEN YOU PASS THROUGH THE WATERS, I WILL BE WITH YOU; AND THROUGH THE RIVERS, THEY SHALL NOT OVERWHELM YOU; WHEN YOU WALK THROUGH FIRE YOU SHALL NOT BE BURNED, AND THE FLAME SHALL NOT CONSUME YOU

Isaiah 43:2

Today's Question

In what area of your life do you feel overwhelmed? Describe the feeling.

_____

_____

_____

_____

_____

_____

_____

_____

Today's Prayer Request

Someone who doesn't believe in Jesus.

"FASTING IS DIRECTED TO TWO THINGS, THE DELETION OF SIN, AND THE RAISING OF THE MIND TO HEAVENLY THINGS."

t.Thomas Aquinas

Today's Question

What have you been excited for lately?

_____

_____

_____

_____

_____

_____

_____

_____

Today's Prayer Request

Someone preparing for a sacrament.

"THE LORD WILL FIGHT FOR YOU, AND YOU HAVE ONLY TO KEEP STILL."

Exodus 14:14

Today's Question

Do you prefer being in a space that is silent or in a place that is loud? Explain.

_____

_____

_____

_____

_____

_____

_____

_____

Today's Prayer Request

Someone who is hungry.

"EVERYTHING IS A REMINDER OF THE CROSS. WE OURSELVES ARE MADE IN THE SHAPE OF A CROSS."

St. John Vianney

Today's Question

How many times do you see a cross or crucifix in your average day? List all the moments.

_____

_____

_____

_____

_____

_____

_____

Today's Prayer Request

Someone who is trying to be a better person.

"FAITH IS TO BELIEVE WHAT YOU DO NOT SEE; THE REWARD OF THIS FAITH IS TO SEE WHAT YOU BELIEVE."

St. Augustine

Today's Question

Do you ever doubt God's existence? What reminds you that he is present?

_____

_____

_____

_____

_____

_____

_____

_____

Today's Prayer Request

Your faith in Jesus to grow.

"DO NOT ABANDON YOURSELVES TO DESPAIR. WE ARE THE EASTER PEOPLE AND HALLELUJAH IS OUR SONG."

St. John Paul II

Made in the USA
Las Vegas, NV
19 February 2024

85945491R00049